FOOTSTEPS

FOOTSTEPS

Poetic reflections on the opposite sex
and Life's other contradictions.

LARRY MORGAN

iUniverse LLC
Bloomington

FOOTSTEPS
Poetic reflections on the opposite sex and Life's other contradictions.

iUniverse books may be ordered through booksellers or by contacting:

iUniverse LLC
1663 Liberty Drive
Bloomington, IN 47403
www.iuniverse.com
1-800-Authors (1-800-288-4677)

Because of the dynamic nature of the Internet, any web addresses or links contained in this book may have changed since publication and may no longer be valid. The views expressed in this work are solely those of the author and do not necessarily reflect the views of the publisher, and the publisher hereby disclaims any responsibility for them.

Any people depicted in stock imagery provided by Thinkstock are models, and such images are being used for illustrative purposes only.
Certain stock imagery © Thinkstock.

ISBN: 978-1-4759-9756-9 (sc)
ISBN: 978-1-4759-9757-6 (ebk)

Printed in the United States of America

iUniverse rev. date: 08/07/2013

This book is dedicated to the women in my life, most of whom treated me better than I deserved.

CONTENTS

RELATIONSHIPS

The best you can hope for in a relationship is to find a
mate whose flaws you can tolerate.

FOOTSTEPS

I'll always be your soul mate,
For our hearts and our minds are as one.
Though cast up on different beaches,
We walk neath the same distant sun.
While separate shores we may wander,
That sun casts its light on the land.
Look over your shoulder beside you,
My footprints you'll see in the sand.

ACHE

I have no plans,
I have nowhere to be.
I have an ache in my heart
That won't let me be.
I feel underfoot,
I seem out of step.
Like a tune out of rhyme,
A conductor inept.
Let's both just back off,
Sort things out for a spell.
Enjoy it here,
I'll just leave for awhile.

ALWAYS NEVER

Always in a hurry,
Always on the go.
Never learned to settle down,
Never could go slow.
Always thought tomorrow
Never held much fright.
Always thought that yesterday
Never worked out right.
Always thought that 'someday'
Never would get here.
Always going somewhere but
Never getting there.
Always meant to tell you,
Never took the time.
Always knew I loved you
Never thought you'd mind.
Always doesn't matter now,
Never fills the air.
Always knew you'd leave someday,
Never knew how much I'd care.

BEATING DEAD HORSES

All we did was argue,
And no one would give in.
Neither of us changed our minds,
So neither one could win.
Round we'd go like jockeys,
Running on a track.
Whipping at each other,
Never giving slack.
We finally had to give it up—
Could not keep up the pace.
Beating on dead horses,
We got scratched from the race.

BREATHLESS

A nosegay lays forlorn,
Cast down on the windowsill.
And the echo of your footsteps,
Can be heard on my stairway still.
The smell of your hair will surround me,
As I turn to your pillow tonight.
But the warmth of your breath will have left me,
As I reach up and turn out the light.
Two AM and I reach for your shoulder—
Roll back as I feel nothing there.
I bury my face in your pillow,
And breathe in the smell of your hair.

CANDLES

How it happened he wasn't quite certain—
Couldn't pin down a date or a place.
But at times everyday he'd remember,
Both the curve of her hips and her face.
Next he'd be saying, "I love you."
And who knows, perhaps it was true.
Words at sixty forgotten—
The saying not easy to do.
And she loved him; she knew it for certain.
Missed his voice and his lips on her face.
But she fought it and all its temptations.
Kept her distance and maintained her space.
In the Fall of his life (she late Summer),
They each felt themselves pinched for time.
Twilight now drawing much nearer,
Both the wax and the wick in decline.
At night, alone, each would consider,
Past mistakes and the things left undone.
Fear is a powerful specter,
So the words simply stuck on their tongues.

CASABLANCA

Snow field shining, pale moon bright,
Blond hair gleaming, wet warm night.
Tangled naked, morning light.
Twilight parting, airplane flight.
Feeling empty, out of sight.
Lonely landing, foggy night.

DARLIN

Let's drop the pretense,
The beat is all gone.
The rhyme and the rhythm
Seem like two different songs.
No longer in sync,
Our tempos have changed.
What used to be hip,
Is a sad old refrain.
Like a tangled up two step
With both partners wrong,
I think it's too late,
To just tango on.
But of all my favorites
From classics to blues,
I have to admit—
There's been no tune like you.

DECISION

It's hard to explain, but I owe it to you.
There's something inside me long hidden from view.
This nagging suspicion that thing's aren't the same.
There's no use in trying to fan the old flame.
The nest is now empty, the children have flown.
In threadbare commitment we find ourselves sewn.
What once was an "us" has become "you" and "me".
With separate lives and diverse destinies.
What passes for passion is really a guise—
Emotionless commitment and soft shallow lies.
I sense this decision we postpone everyday—
Do we stay together, or go separate ways?

FRESH CUT FLOWERS

Fresh cut flowers,
A contradiction in terms.
Love and its vigor
Turn quickly infirm.
Nipped in the bud,
Or left on the vine.
Romance, like flowers,
Can wither in time.

GOING THRU THE MOTIONS

We're going through the motions
Of going through our lives.
Like planets locked in orbit,
Like stars in desert skies.
What passes now for choices,
Is really just a guise.
Emotionless commitment,
And regulated sighs.

HE NEVER SAID THAT HE COULD FLY

He never said that he could fly.
He only said you'd touch the sky.
He never said that he could sing.
He only said you'd hear bells ring.

He never said that he could dance.
He only said you'd be entranced.
He never said he was the best.
He only said he'd take your test.

He never said he knew your heart.
He only said he'd take your part.
He never said there'd be no cold.
He only said he's yours to hold.

He never said there'd be no fears.
He only said he'd dry your tears.
He never said, its smooth, this road.
He only said he'd share your load.

Now what he said and what he does,
No longer seem to earn your love.
So many things that might have been,
Appear in sight but fade again.

The roads he chose were often wrong.
His path grew steep, the drop was long.
Out on the edge up there so high.
I bet he wishes he could fly.

HEARTS IN MOTION

She found he wasn't perfect,
So he no longer tried.
They both stopped chasing rainbows,
That once lit up their skies.
Where once they both saw sunshine,
They both saw only rain.
What sounded like a chorus,
Became a sad refrain.
They stuck it out for years and years,
As if trapped in a maze.
But after wasting all that time
They went their separate ways.
I wonder if they find it sad,
Reflecting on their loss.
And maybe even tragic,
When they added up the cost.
So when you first discover,
Your heart's not really in it.
Don't just go through the motions,
Instead just up and quit it.

ICK ON YOU

I'll never get the ick on you,
I don't know how to hate.
Even when you're old and gray,
Or start to pack on weight.
Through thick and thin I'll stand by you,
For better or for worse.
And when you take that final gasp,
I'll be your final nurse.

But if your eye should wander,
Or god forbid you stray.
Best ponder life without me . . .
Cause I'll be on my way.

LITTLE LIES

Little lies
In little places.
Compromises,
Brief embraces.
Turn by turn
The knot was tied.
Twist by twist
The lie was lied.
What remains
When we're undone?
What's the total?
What's the sum?
We always pick
The easy way.
And pay the price
And walk away.

ONE NIGHT STAND

A cheap motel with one night stand,
A bed and no TV.
I don't know how we got there,
It still amazes me.
We'd chatted over drinks,
Somehow the time just flew.
I had just turned thirty,
I guessed you forty two.
Older woman, younger man,
That's how the story goes.
Keeping our pretenses,
But shedding all our clothes.
Twenty years have come and gone,
And other women too.
But I still see that one night stand,
And I still think of you.

POINTS OF LIGHT

The desert sky fell silent,
As two lovers lie tangled in dreams.
The plans and the schemes of tomorrow,
Were postponed for far better things.
As their warm breath commingled about them,
The moon on the sand dune slipped low.
With their bodies entwined ever tighter,
Their lips touched in sweet afterglow.
Are the stars in the sky really beacons,
Or just points of light cast astray?
Do our hearts really beat as one person,
Or is passion the cosmos at play?
When we wake in the cold light of morning,
Will our souls merge as one with the dawn?
Or will we, like the stars of the evening,
Just fade with the sun and be gone?

QUICKIE

Only have a minute.
Even less time yesterday.
Busy doing other things,
Just working my life away.
But it only takes a second,
To say a word or two.
I'll always find the time,
To say that I love you.

TANGO

The steps we dance are strange,
Me and my ex wife.
Patterned choreography,
Not good but not quite strife.
Never in each others life,
But never really out.
Interlopers each we are,
Pensive, both in doubt.
Into the night we contemplate,
Our solo symphonies.
Silhouettes in moonlight,
But just from memory.
Tangled in a glistening web,
But somehow both set free.
The path ahead not easy,
But one that has to be.

TIME AND SPACE

The steps you dance are strange,
You and your recent ex.
Patterned choreography,
A nervous throbbing itch.

Never quite together,
Since one of you moved out.
Interlopers each you are,
Pensive, both in doubt.

Each singing in the night,
Their solo symphonies.
Silhouettes on moonlight,
But just from memory.

Tangled in a lonely web,
Anchored at the heart.
Trapped in time together,
Locked in space apart.

TWILIGHT COMET

Perhaps the heat from distant light,
Is sent by cosmic wind.
The sun reflected by the moon,
Reflects upon our skin.
Caught up by some great gravity,
Two objects locked in place.
In orbit for eternity,
We have our niche in space.
One comet in a life time,
Is more than most observe.
One lover in our twilight,
Is more than most deserve.

UNFINISHED LOVE SONG

First touch first embrace and first passion,
The lyrics flowed easy and fast.
The melody played like a trumpet,
Each chorus as good as the last.
At first the words came so easy.
It wasn't a hard thing to do.
Caught up in the moment and magic,
The notes and the melody true.
It's strange how what seems like forever,
Can suddenly take a wrong turn.
A word or a glance or a comment,
And bridges are suddenly burned.
Perhaps our love song is over.
Perhaps it fades out like the sun.
Perhaps we compose it anew.
Perhaps we just leave it undone.
But there's little time left to start over,
And less just to waste keeping time.
We're trapped in iambic indifference,
A couple who no longer rhyme.

US IN LITTLE WORDS

And silly me
Thinking of you
Thinking of us
Each with walls
Then with windows
Looking back
Looking away
Looking out
Looking in
Seeking
Sorting
Doubting
Risking
Touching
Feeling
Sensuous
Tactile
Moist
Compelling silly me to think of us
In little words.

WORDS IN WAITING

To me her eyes were heaven,
As their gaze about me fell.
And I saw there in them shining,
The words I longed to tell.
A boy and girl in Summer,
Each just turned sixteen.
Pressed against a tall oak tree,
In a woods both dark and green.
Your first real love I'm certain,
Is one you don't forget.
Moist throbbing aching passion,
With no thoughts of regret.
But first loves like the snow of Spring,
Intended not to last.
Remembered now so vividly,
Though so far in the past.
Many years have come and gone,
And lovers just as well.
I find myself still waiting,
For the words I long to tell.

WOMEN

There are only two ways to deal with women, but nobody knows
either one of them.

CHANGE OF LIFE

Morning's first sunshine too soon became noon,
Afternoon's shadows gave way to the moon.
You busied yourself, as best as you could,
And promised yourself it was all for the good.
But yesterday's mirror seemed somehow more kind.
Today's lines are clearer and easy to find.
The day you turned thirty you stayed twenty-nine.
But now you've turned fifty in such a short time.
Spring is long gone, and summer's not near,
With winter so close you can feel it from here.
The print on the page and the future not clear.
Things out of fashion that you still hold dear.
Where has it gone and what will remain?
Where are the victories and where is the gain?
Life is a circle that has but two sides—
Just inside and outside with no place to hide.

DAUGHTERS

When I was just a girl of ten,
All my friends would say.
That I was like my mother,
And I'd be her some day.
Now my mother's eighty-five,
Her birthday was today.
But she has lost her daughter,
Her mind has lost it's way.
Her memories are all but gone,
I don't think she can rally.
The twists and turns of life,
Left her up a blind alley.
Lost in her amnesia,
A hopeless situation.
She stares at me but draws a blank,
I stare back in frustration.
When I look at my mother,
Can that be me I see?
A glimpse into my future,
And what I'll one day be?
But I don't have a daughter,
Like me to care for me.
And now she doesn't either,
She can't remember me.
I'm reminded back when I was ten,
And all my friends would say.
That I was like my mother,
And I'd be her some day.

EASY

A pretty girl is like,
A melody they say.
The image in your mind,
Can linger night and day.
So easy on the eyes,
You love them from the start,
But then they end up being,
So hard on your heart.

FORGET IT

Women always worry about,
The things that I forget.
Birthdays' and anniversaries,
Have caused me much regret.
I don't care much about a thing,
She forgot back in September.
What causes all my problems are,
The things that she remembers.

GIFTING

Your birthday is here and I ponder,
Just what sort of gift to give you.
We live on different levels,
And don't share the same point of view.
About you the thing that attracts me,
You haven't the slightest of clues.
Your stocks may well triple in value,
But the best thing that you own is you.
Wealth's a selfish and seductive power,
But robs us of love in the end.
While saving up great stores of money,
It's your time you most wastefully spend.
So what sort of gift for a female,
Bedecked in diamonds and furs?
Who lies in her bed every morning,
Surrounded by treasures d' jour.
I've always been partial to flowers.
I don't mean the store bought kind.
I'm sure that you'll get those from others.
This bouquets a gift from my mind.

GRAVITY

Isaac Newton figured out
Why apples fall from trees.
This universal law it seems,
Applies to you and me.
What goes up someday comes down,
A fact of life for certain.
All actors strut upon the stage,
But face a falling curtain.
And so it is with breasts I guess,
Though surgeons make them perfect.
They sit there high and mighty,
And look just plain terrific.
But then that Isaac Newton thing,
Begins to take effect,
And all the parts around them,
Soon show signs of neglect.
A sagging chin, a wrinkled brow
As flesh heads earthward bound.
Those breasts may still be perfect,
But men just don't come round.
For God's sake give your breasts a break,
They have a right to sag.
Eighty and with perfect breasts?
It's enough to make you gag.
So ladies leave your tits alone,
Don't lift or spread or bob em.
Given up on having sex?
Now there's the real problem!

ODDS ARE

A sweet young thing named Sarah,
Was searching for a mate.
And found she had exhausted,
The lower forty-eight.
So North she turned to try her luck,
In the land of midnight sun.
In hopes that she could find at last,
That one and only one.
To her delight when she got there,
The place was full of guys.
And hardly any females so
Her hopes were running high.
But all the men she dated,
Were wearing flannel shirts.
Their long and scruffy beards,
Were wild and full of dirt.
They took a bath, well, now and then.
And drove a beat up truck.
Lived in the woods and came to town,
Each month to try their luck.
Indeed she was surrounded,
By manly rugged men.
And every night she had her pick,
She scored and scored again.
She found out that the odds were good,
Indeed twas fertile sod.
But soon she left Alaska,
Cause all the goods were odd.

OUT ON A LIMB

Birds of feather, all flocked together,
Wheel through the amber sky.
They twist and turn in unison,
Choreographed they fly.
Alas a tiny feathered speck,
Goes left as all turn right.
The others never taking note
Are quickly out of sight.
The single bird flies overhead,
Into the setting sun.
Confident in solitude,
She is a flock of one.

RABBIT HABIT

Rabbits come in many forms,
In colors shapes and sizes.
They satisfy a lady's needs,
Indulging her sweet vices.
Factories run into the night,
Avoiding sexual crisis.
In fact the Rabbit leads all sales,
Of vibrating devices.
It made its name, you may recall,
Twas in Sex And The City.
They did an intervention,
Her addiction wasn't pretty.
It won't leave up the toilet seat,
And you don't have to feed it.
It never strays or drinks too much,
The night stand nicely keeps it.
It never says you are too fat,
It has no thoughts to guess.
It's there right when you need it.
And never leaves a mess.
It twists and turns and pulses,
Its kind of cute to view.
And unlike men who are such dogs,
It really loves just you.

But something's missing woman like,
In pleasures they can savor.
With little ears and rings of pearls,
It ought to come in flavors.
And so it was great chefs conspired,
To give the Rabbit flavor.
They searched the land and tried to find,
The taste that women favor.
They tried liqueurs of every kind,
Then lamb and ham and turkey.
What flavor will the rabbit be?
You guessed it . . .its beef jerky!

SHADOW WOMAN

Wrapped in a shawl
From the sun or the cold,
She shuffles along,
The essence of old.
Worn shoes scuff her path
With the aid of a cane.
Hunch backed and poor
No one knows her name.
Her mate now long gone,
A life spent in sorrow.
The children don't call,
It's an empty tomorrow.
The days that remain,
End in nights spent alone.
No friends come around
And no chats on the phone.
I wonder sometimes,
As I see her pass by.
Would I so endure?
Or just give up and die?
As she slips out of sight
I conclude with a sigh . . .
The golden years are
One hell of a lie.

SHE

Pages in a woman's life,
Look for love and roll the dice.
Meet a man, now She's a wife.
Feel some bliss, endure some strife.
Raise the kids to be their best.
Suddenly an empty nest.
Marriage doesn't stand the test.
She's divorced just like the rest.
She's out in the single scene.
Meeting guys with twisted schemes.
Men who hide their wedding ring,
One night stands and weekend flings.
Girlfriend chatter on the phone,
She spends lots of time alone.
In a house not quite a home.
Thinking how the years have flown.
She meets the girls for lunch at noon,
Takes the dog and gets him groomed.
Tennis in the afternoon.
Cocktail time comes way to soon.
One nice guy, She has a date.
Call him back or should she wait?
Wondering, is it too late?
Forever single seems her fate.
In the mirror can that be She?
Aging lines so plain to see.
Not the gal She used to be.
Oh my God. I think She's me!

SIX IN THE MORNING

White cotton panties,
Red blushing face.
Transparent bra,
Ribbons and lace.
Soft velvet blouse,
Wispy blond hair.
Blue denim jeans,
Shaped like a pear.
Hand on my collar,
Tongue in my ear.
Can't open my eyes–
You might disappear.
Is it all for real
Or only a scheme?
Don't want to wake up
If it's just a dream.
Make of this title
Whatever you may.
Stay in my dreams
Or come out and play.

TABLE FOR TWO

"How'd it go today dear",
She asked as he came through the door.
"Fine," he said as he turned on
The TV to check out the scores.
Needing adult conversation,
After spending all day with the kids,
She busied herself in the kitchen,
And pondered the one word he'd said.
"What's for dinner?" he muttered,
As he opened a bottle of beer.
"Corned beef and cabbage", she answered.
He turned up his nose in a sneer.
Setting the food on the table,
She carefully turned down the lights.
He scarcely looked up from the paper—
"Where are the kids tonight?"
"They're spending the night with mother."
The candles she lit then poured wine.
"How does it look?" she inquired.
He sat down and simply said, "fine".
He wolfed down his dinner in silence,
Never once looking up at his mate.
Then left her alone at the table.
Dejected, she stared at her plate.
Tomorrow he'd find the house empty.
He'd wake up alone with the dawn.
She'd wonder if he'd ever miss her,
Or even know why she had gone.

THAR SHE BLOWS . . . NOT!

The day she said "I do"
She really meant I don't.
It didn't mean she couldn't,
It simply meant she won't.
Back when you were dating,
She did a glorious thing,
That she no longer has to do
Cause she now wears your ring.
I'm talking about blow jobs,
A thing she did each day.
Now even if you beg and plead,
She'll simply say "no way."
Occasionally she may give in,
But it won't be too often.
Guys tell me that their birthday was
The last time that they got one.
Recall this little poem
As yours walks down the aisle,
For it explains the reason she,
Is wearing a big smile.

TIGHTROPE

Black Widow spider,
Weaves a fine web.
Soft moonlight glistens,
On delicate threads.

Casting a shadow,
And temping his fate.
He senses the danger,
Of being her mate.

Dancing on tightropes,
She greets the new dawn.
The sun has now risen,
But he is all gone.

VAPOR

Comet streaking through the night,
Vaporized by sun star light.
Captured in eternal flight,
Streaking one day out of sight.
Maiden smiling in the night,
Glowing as by comets light.
Contemplating thoughts of flight,
Lingering still but out of sight.

WHO YOU ARE

You compel me to prose
Words like casual clothes
softly flow.
In the dark of the night
By word processors light
Here they go.
You don't know who I am
And I can't guess your plan
Does it show?
In a sea cast adrift
With no port in your midst
Caught in tow.
Like a bird lost from sight
As she ponders her plight
And her woes.
I've been there myself,
Lived my life on a shelf,
Felt alone.
Its not easy to stay—
Or to just run away.
Yes, I know who you are.

REAL MEN

All men break women's hearts, real men put them back together.

BLINDERS

Gazing at a woman's breasts,
Is like looking at the sun.
To stare more than a second,
You should put sunglasses on.

CHORES

Would you come and help weed my garden?
It's long overgrown from neglect.
Where once bloomed a row of petunias,
Weeds now stand in clumps circumspect.
And maybe you'd clean out my closet.
My clothes aren't in style anymore.
What once draped a man in his forties,
Now hides in the dark behind doors.
And maybe you'd fill up my pantry.
It once brimmed with wonderful fare.
I no longer open that door much,
It pains me to see it so bare.
I know that my kitchen is lacking,
In tools that bring meals to life.
I mostly eat out now in restaurants,
Alone midst the husbands and wives.
It's hard for a man in his sixties,
Left with reflections and thoughts,
To share his emotions and feelings—
To let down his guard and get caught.
So let's just forget that I asked you.
I'm sure that you have other plans.
If this sort of thing were you're calling,
You'd already be with a man.

COWBOY

You always were my hero
When I was just a pup.
A real Wyoming cowboy,
As I was growing up.
I'd often sit and listen
To stories and to songs.
"Here's one my Uncle told to me,"
I'd say and pass it on.
Now I am a grown man,
Though not as wise as you.
And you are still my hero,
From every point of view.
I never can repay your gifts,
Some old and some brand new.
And when I'm at my very best,
It's all because of you.

DOUBLE PLAY

Its midnight on the red-eye
At thirty thousand feet.
I'm off to see the playoffs'
In first class leather seats.
My father was a baseball fan,
That's how I learned the game.
A common man of no renown,
He had no wealth or fame.
His lessons and his memory,
Are with me here tonight.
It's our last chance to win it all,
And his first airplane flight.
He doesn't have a ticket,
But he's on board just the same.
And tomorrow when they yell, "play ball,"
He'll be there at the game.

HE NEVER

He never wrote her a poem,
Words just weren't his style.
Flowers and gifts weren't his forte,
And they hadn't held hands in awhile.
But he loved her and that was for certain.
But she left him cause she never knew.
And now she's got a new lover,
Who does the things he didn't do.

HUNG

My ex once had a boyfriend,
In days of long gone by.
Whose tool was big enough she said,
To make a grown horse cry.
And all her girlfriends knew it
(You know how girls will talk.)
I guess he was a legend,
With that enormous cock.
Can't ask her what he looked like,
She can't recall his face.
But astronauts could see his thing
From up in outer space.
Well I can lick my eyebrows,
And breathe through both my ears.
I guess that's why he lost her,
And why she called me "dear."
Eventually we parted,
It wasn't meant to be.
Because it seems she never,
Acquired a taste for me!

I MAILED IT TOMORROW

I mailed it tomorrow,
Didn't have any time left today.
I was busy out running some errands,
(Busy wasting my life away.)
But I thought of you oh so often.
And I wondered "What's new with you?"
So I mailed it tomorrow,
When I had nothing better to do.
Tomorrow's a wonderful feeling,
Full of promise of good things to come.
So I thought—I'll just mail it tomorrow.
(But I don't really know just which one.)

KATZ

Newkie barely gets about,
He's seventeen, this cat.
No tabby this old timer,
He's black and that is that.
Sometimes he stares into space.
Now and then he purrs.
Mostly he just sleeps a lot.
Sometimes he licks his fur.
His life had not been easy,
Survival was a chore.
He'd never been the alpha cat,
And lived behind closed doors.
Then one day I rescued him,
And down the road we sped.
Like Harry and old Tonto,
Our jailor we both shed.
And now these are his golden years,
Rescued just in time.
At last he has a home that's his,
He naps in warm sunshine.
I guess I'm kinda like this cat,
No longer in my prime.
We syncopate together,
In Catatonic time.

LAST MAN CLUB

The old men at the party,
Each and all were buddies.
Their faces lined and faded
As the combat maps once studied.
A last man's club near midnight,
Their numbers growing small.
No longer straight and sturdy,
No longer brave and tall.
Each raised his glass to soldiers,
Now harder to remember.
With tearful eye and heavy heart,
All now in late December.
We're all in a last man's club,
As agile youth grows feeble.
Each and every hundred years,
It's almost all new people.

LIVING WITH ME

Living me with me must have been a frustration.
Took all the wrong turns at my own invitation.
Usually gave in to my worst inclinations.
It seems like I never stayed home.
Thinking back now bout our last conversation,
My overblown ego and dumb proclamations.
How did I waste all your sweet dedication?
Why didn't I just stay home?
I was too blind to see plain revelation.
Now that you're gone it's my constant fixation.
Realize now you were my one salvation.
I can't seem to find my way home.
Threw love away without contemplation.
Too late in life for such sad consternation.
I made the worst of a good situation.
Too late now to find my way home.

OLD LEAF

Caught on the fence
Like a leaf in the gale.
There's no going forward,
I'm snagged in full sail.
From soft sunny bough,
To cold jagged steel.
My path indirect
With frequent ordeals.
From April to Autumn,
The seasons were spent.
Just hanging around,
To my sad lament.
Now withered and tattered,
I twist in the wind.
With winter upon me
And no time to mend.

ONE DAY SHY

One day shy of February 1968,
He's in the town of Hue.
They'll call it "Tet Offensive"
In the history books someday.
This is such a humid place,
Mud red and forest green.
Not the place he wants to be,
But he's a young Marine.
Tracers light the pre-dawn sky,
The Perfume River flows.
By evening it will be blood red,
Some guys won't make it home.
I thought this was a holiday,
Charlie said he would stand down.
Now the lyin slant eyed prick,
Is shootin up the town.
In Nam just shy of thirteen months,
He's supposed to leave today.
How'd this fuckin happen?
He's here and in harms way.
He's one day shy of twenty-one,
Will he see twenty-two?
Or even see tomorrow,
I think they've broken thru.

He never heard the bullet,
Or saw the shooters face.
He never felt his heart explode,
Or knew he'd left this place.
Back home the hippies fill the streets,
The Generals all lied.
He's one day shy no longer.
On Tet day one he died.

PARTNERS

Dawn breaks in Wyoming,
On a cabin and a boat.
A splash of water and they're off.
Two pals are set afloat.
Locked on point he stands there,
A fixed and silent stare.
A look back at his partner,
Then feathers fill the air.
The campfire circle tightens,
Good buddies gather round.
Most sit on chairs or benches,
But one lies on the ground.
How long has it been pal,
Since on this trip we started?
All those roads and all those miles,
And never once we parted.
It's time to say goodbye now,
We knew this day would come.
But someday we will meet again.
And I will watch you run.
Life can be so perfect
If two can share a plan.
Partners on the an open road.
A truck. A dog. A man.

REUNION

Hot summer nights entwined neath the stars,
Your first taste of me in the back of dad's car.
Moist secret places explored and discovered,
Taking you home and dodging your mother.
Too early in life we discovered each other,
Never were friends but always were lovers.
Then took separate paths away from each other,
Made real friends and found different lovers.
I came back home for this class reunion,
Hoping to see you and check out your new one.
Nothing has changed and you don't look older.
(I know it's a lie but that's what I told her.)

SENTRIES

It was moonlight on snow; it was twenty below,
And the Wyoming cold settled in.
The night was so chilled that the star twinkle stilled
In the air dry as martini gin.
I sat there alone, in that place I called home,
And I gazed through a frost-covered pane.
There were trees standing guard, with their limbs frozen hard,
At attention all night they'd remain.
The moon was so bright, you could read by its light,
And the cold made the house creek and moan.
To that pane I was drawn, till the sun met the dawn,
Finding me sitting there all alone.
In defeat I have fled, from that climate so dread,
And it seems like a long time ago.
When I sat there that night, in the eerie moonlight,
With those sentries alone in the snow.

SOMETIMES THE WORDS WON'T COME

Sometimes the words won't come,
And you feel like you've just run dry.
Sometimes they come so easy,
From mind to paper they fly.
It's mostly just digging them out.
From the shadows of your mind.
Or simply just making them up—
Finding spontaneous rhyme.
What do you do with a world of words
That spin inside your head?
They either find an exit,
Or remain unborn—unsaid.
And so it is with life,
(If you share my point of view.)
Perhaps our only failures,
Lie in what we do not do.

SPLIT DECISION

Sooner or latter
She'll demand a decision.
Its time for commitment
Or total recession.
The decision is easy.
It comes down to a question.
The answer to which
You'll deduce on reflection.
Just ask yourself this
If you're pondering a wedding;
Is the fucking you're getting
Worth the fucking you're getting?

LIFE

Life is what happened to the plan we started out with.

ACCOUNTING 101

The greatest gifts, not easily lost,
Are those from the heart—regardless of cost.
Mere words on paper, a rhyme or a tune,
Remind us of summer and things done too soon.
We count our possessions and things left undone.
Then total the numbers in search of a sum.
In dollars and cents all fortunes are small.
Life, love, and friendship account for it all.
Neath warm summer skies we glide down life's stream.
As we near the end it seems but a dream.
The greatest things we gave to each other
Were gifts of ourselves, not those cross the counter.

BORROWED TIME

There's no paying back now
The years we've been lent.
Less time left ahead
Than we've already spent.
It's a curious fact
That we all face someday.
It was all borrowed time
And it's all the same day.

BOTH SIDES NOW

The grass is always greener . . .
At least that's what we're told.
But colors start to fade a bit,
As we grow wise and old.
I spent years of climbing,
Through walls of wood and wire.
Of looking for that greener grass,
I never seemed to tire.
Perhaps I should have questioned,
Those sayings from the start.
Cause it's too soon that we grow old,
And too late we grow smart.
At last I have discovered,
That old saying made no sense.
The grass is really greener,
On BOTH sides of the fence.

BURN OUT

Every fire is different
No matter how it burns.
No matter how the fire may blaze,
Or how the flames may turn.
Hypnotized we sit and watch,
The colors and the hues.
The red and orange and scarlet,
The indigo and blue.
Eventually the fire burns out,
No indigo or blue.
A final flicker then its gone.
Just like me and you.

CALL WAITING

It's not much of a deal,
A decision quite small.
I've stopped calling people
Who don't return calls.
I guess they were busy.
But I'm busy too.
And if you can't call me . . .
Then I won't call you.
I'm amazed at the time,
That it saves me each day.
I've got more time to think,
And more time to play.
And more time to search out,
And more chance to find.
Clients and friends,
Who want to be mine.

CAR BUFF

Objects in the mirror
May in fact be nearer
Than they look.
That old man staring back,
May in point of fact,
Be just how you look.
The off ramp goes but one way
In life, as on the freeway,
We all must exit someday.

CHOICES ARE

Choices are . . .
Decisions we make everyday.
Do we stay and fight our own battles,
Or turn tail and just run away.
Left or right at main street?—
Which sweater goes with these slacks?
Paper or plastic or something fantastic
Go forward or should I turn back?
We worry and fret over big things.
As if we had chance to make sway.
The big moves in life were decided,
By the small ones we made yesterday.

CLIPPED FOR TIME

The old man in the barber chair,
Had weathered skin and silver hair.
The glass reflected hollow eyes.
A mirrored image compromised.
Reflecting mostly on the past,
Would this haircut be his last?
I wondered as I watched him there—
When would I take up his chair?

DANCER

Life is really pure ballet,
A dance upon a stage.
We walk about on tippy toe,
A prancer in a cage.
Unseen eyes behind the lights,
Watch us and they gauge.
We pirouette and strut about,
And then we leave the stage.
Too soon our dance is over,
Our part it seems was small.
At last we take our final bow,
There is no curtain call.

DOG STYLE

The dog raced in a circle,
And chased his tail around,
Never ever catching up,
Or even gaining ground.
I know just how that poor pup feels,
All caught up in a race.
Chasing things I never catch—
But somehow keeping pace.

FLIGHT OF THOUGHT

A rain forest trip I took one day,
Sun filtered thru the trees.
The path meandered in the mist,
A butterfly followed me.
Erratic but with purpose,
Those purple wings did beat.
I stopped there as it fluttered.
And soon I fell asleep.
I dreamed I was a butterfly,
As I slept neath a tree.
The butterfly then feel asleep,
And dreamed that he was me.
Then we awoke together,
Still tangled in our dream.
Both sitting there as one.
Or so it seemed to be.
Rain forest man or butterfly,
Tell me reader if you can.
Am I a dreaming butterfly?
Or just a sleepy man?

GOING DOWN?

Someday we will all be gone,
No matter who we are.
The down and out, the middle class,
The famous movie star.
Life's journey is a one-way trip,
An elevator ride.
Encapsulated friends and foes,
Descending side by side.
We crowd aboard and choose our floor,
All caught up in the race.
But the buttons pushed don't matter
Cause we end up in the same place.

HELLO GOODBYE

Of all the things we do in life,
I think I have discovered.
The thing we do the worst,
We do to one another.
Hello is rather easy.
We say it when we meet.
We say it on the telephone.
We say it on the street.
Goodbye is something different.
Endings are not easy.
Filled with much uncertainty,
They leave us feeling queasy.
Athletes wait far too long.
Politicians even longer.
The urge to leave is there,
But the urge to stay is stronger.

HIGHER BEING

God answers all prayers
Though sometimes the answer comes slow.
Sometimes the answer is maybe
And sometimes the answer is no.

HINDSIGHT

Looking back on the road ahead,
I see all the mistakes. I feel all the dread.
The turns I took and ways I went astray.
Opportunities missed each step of the way.
Men past their prime don't recall the gains.
They remember the failure and re-feel the pain.
It isn't just death that they all fear at last.
It's the fear of the failures in their future and past.

HOME ALONE

Silence echoed down the hall,
No footfalls sounded large or small.
The wooden hill stood waiting there,
For shoes to tread upon the stair.
No slamming door or ringing phone.
No playful pup to chew his bone.
Empty now and all alone—
A waiting house with no one home.

IN TIME

Death comes.
The final giving back.
To the earth.
To the universe
To God.
All we began as and became.
The fleshy parts.
To star stuff.
A flicker of light.
Extinguished.
Unnoticed amidst the bonfire that is the cosmos.
I am mortal.
I will die.
I will be gone.
I will not see the sun
Or hear the lark
Or feel the spark
Of life.
Ever again.

LEGACY

The child you were yesterday and the parent you will become
Are the same adult you are today.
Your teachers were the children of their childhood.
They were the adults of your childhood.
They helped form the chains from which you hang today's anchors.
We are thus festooned.
Scarcely recalling our anchorless days.
The forging so incremental
But the anchors are always our own.
And the chains from which they hang always our own.
And the choice to remain there moored always our own.
Your child, unanchored but aware
Will learn by observation, that an anchor he must bear.
All the freedom or frustration that eventually he'll sample
Will not come from contemplation
He will learn it by example.

MORE OR LESS?

The more that we acquire, the more we have to lose.
And further down the road we find less exits left to choose.
This seeming contradiction is ultimately fate.
Life is full of tradeoffs, unknown till its too late.
We trade our time for money, and buy all sorts of things;
A bigger house, a better car, a brighter diamond ring.
Then finally when we're out of time we find it a bit sad.
We traded what we really want for what we always had.

NOMADS

Travelers all in transit,
I guess I've seen em all.
From Motel 6 to Hilton,
From Sydney to Sioux Falls.
Down and out or wealthy,
Big bucks or getting by.
Some are on a budget,
Some are flying high.
Some show up in limos,
Others come by cab.
Some pay up with crumpled cash,
Others run a tab.
Different as we may be,
Entourage or all alone.
We have one thing in common,
We wish that we were home.

OLD BEGINNINGS

Are these just old beginnings?
Have we passed this way before?
Headed off in a former direction—
Like waves on their usual shore.
Is this journey somehow different?
A pathway untried but true.
A whole new adventure for certain,
On a heading exciting and new.
No matter what the outcome,
It's always a mighty tough call.
The trouble with a sure thing is
The uncertainty of it all.

PENTAMETER

It's time to change pentameter
When the old one doesn't fit.
It's time to seek a different style,
The former one to quit.
In life as well as poetry,
It's just your point of view.
Why not simply start today
To be the real you.
The sun will rise, the sun will set,
No matter what we do.
But all the choices in between
Are up to me and you.

PHOENIX

Endless byways
Desert heat.
Boys of summer
Flying feet.
Child in waiting
Time to go.
Concrete ribbon
Sunset glow.
Through desert sky
A comet roams
A lucky Phoenix
Heading home.
Life's a circle
Nothing new
A lucky me
A lucky you.

PICTURES ON THE BABY GRAND

Pictures facing outward,
Sit on the baby grand.
Family, friends and lovers,
Glass covered there they stand.
Memories of days gone by,
And lives now gone as well.
Captured there forever,
Each face a story tells.
What becomes of faces,
Trapped inside a frame?
When their keeper passes,
And no one knows their names.
They sit inside an antique store,
Orphans now at last.
Anonymous, collecting dust,
Staring thru a glass.

PLAYBALL!

It's just a game we call baseball.
Nine men playing out in the sun.
It seems like a simple endeavor;
Of throw, catch, hit and then run.
We call it the "national pastime",
From memories of earlier days.
When boys and their fathers took time off,
To come out and watch grown men play.
Many consider it boring.
They don't understand how to wait.
Nine chess pieces out on a field.
One batsman alone at the plate.
There's no other game just like baseball.
With no other sport does it fit.
The contest could go on forever—
There's no clock to tell us to quit.
The man with the ball? He plays defense.
Most men on the offense sit down.
An umpire judges each motion.
The manager paces and frowns.
Baseball can be a real heartbreak.
But that suits the real fan just fine.
Each game is in doubt 'til it's over.
The best teams may lose half the time.

A hero must put up with failure,
Each season brings errors to mind.
And even the greatest of hitters,
Succeeds just 3 out of 10 tries.
Owners spend millions of dollars,
And players spend all of their prime.
But the fan is the one who's the winner,
Of the game played on grass in sunshine.

REMEMBRANCE

I remember my teacher.
She was hired by the Board,
Paid for by the levy,
And licensed by the state.
She existed in the very womb of democracy.
Midwife to a generation
Whose gestation lasted
Nine months.
She was a controller;
Of stiff necks
And straight backs
And eyes glazed over.
She had a particular expertise:
She crushed dreams
And broke spirits
For four thousand dollars a month.

RETIRED

I wake up in the morning,
I fall asleep at night.
Each day the hours in between,
Tick slowly out of sight.
Every day just like the last,
A string of yesterdays.
No different than tomorrow,
The same in every way.
Can't think about the future,
Or contemplate the past.
Monotony has gotten me,
Trapped with this plot and cast.
It seems I'm in a movie,
Or repetitious play.
I feel just like Bill Murray.
I'm stuck in groundhog day!

SCORE CARD

Life's a game like baseball,
It's played between the lines.
With lots of people keeping score,
But no one keeping time.
Some days you win, some days you lose,
And some days it is raining.
You may well know the inning,
But not the time remaining.

SEPARATE WAYS

A farm dog and a wolf,
Were walking down a lane.
The wolf was lean and wild,
The farm dog fat and tame.

"Tell me wolf," the farm dog asked,
"How do you spend your days?
What do you do for food,
At night where do you stay?"

Wolf said, "I hunt for food,
Some times I do not eat.
A den inside a hill,
Is where I usually sleep.

I search for food all night,
I try to sleep all day.
My enemies are many,
On guard I have to stay.

And then the wolf inquired,
"Are your days just like mine?
Do you sleep in a den,
And eat what you can find?"

"No," the farm dog answered,
"It's not like that at all.
I never have to hunt,
I sleep on fresh clean straw.

Nothing try's to harm me,
The farmer treats me well.
I hang around the yard,
Then hear the dinner bell.

Why not come home with me?
You' never have to work.
We'd lay around all day,
And share in all the perks."

Then the wolf inquired,
"Of us what does he ask?
For his generosity,
He must require a task."

Dog said, "it's so easy,
Just wear a collar everyday."
Hearing that the wolf turned round,
And ran the other way.

THE DOWNHILL SIDE OF FIFTY

The downhill side of Fifty,
I thought I'd never see it.
But when the weathers damp and cold
I sure as hell can feel it.
The downhill side of fifty.
Not yet the "golden years".
Not young or old, just in between,
With vision not too clear.
The downhill side of fifty,
What can you do about it?
Too late to start all over,
But still too soon to quit.

TIME

No time left for lessons learned.
No time left for lovers spurned.
No time left for bridges burned.
No time left for money earned.
Winter tugs upon my sleeve,
Friends pass on and take their leave.
Their memories a tapestry weave.
Sometimes I smile, sometimes I grieve.

UP STREAM

Ever on and ever on
Up the stream from dawn to dawn
Dodging, darting, leaping falls,
Answering primordial calls.
Are we so different when it's done?
For when the race is finally run,
We all end up back in the sea—
Endless salmon endless me.

WHOSE KILLING WHOM?

Killing time is something,
You really shouldn't do.
Cause you're not killing time,
It's time that's killing you!

WIND AND SAND

Long ago the caravans
Made their marks upon these sands.
Man on beast like ships would glide
On seas of sand the wind they'd ride.
With flowing robes and turbans tight
Across the dunes and out of sight.
We too must cover up our skin,
And ride our beasts of glass and tin.
As seekers now we come again,
To make our tracks and feel the wind.
Before we leave this timeless place,
The sun will warm and brown our face.
The heat will fade; the night will chill,
And stars will light the dunes so still.
Dead soldiers dot the bleak landscape,
A higher court has sealed their fate.
Shifting sands though endless times,
An eerie silence drains my mind.
The past is looted. What remains?
What's the cost and what's the gain?
We too are but mere grains of sand,
Moved about as if by plan.
We too must pass—we cannot stay.
And the wind will blow our tracks away.

HUMOR

Laughter might just be the most important thing to put on
your bucket list.

BOOMER

You'll not pitch for the Yankees,
Or be the President.
Or write that one great novel,
Or compose a top ten hit.
Those boyhood dreams won't happen,
It's mighty plain to see.
A freight train named old age,
Is headed straight for thee.
Those years went by so quickly,
And in the mirror you see,
A wrinkled face and thinning hair.
Who can that old man be?
Your clothes are not in fashion,
Your music out of style.
Young girls look right thru you,
And never flash a smile.
Like all the other "boomers"
Your pensions way too small.
The days go by in solitude,
You wander through the mall.
If you could do it over,
But know what you know now.
You'd buy Microsoft at 15 bucks.
Your life would be a "wow".

You wouldn't marry Doris,
Your backseat high school flame.
Or fight that war in Viet Nam.
Things wouldn't be the same.
You'd write that one great novel,
Compose that top ten hit.
The Yankees would have signed you,
And you'd be President.
But time is like a freeway,
Except there is no map.
You're kind of feeling sleepy now . . .
Why not just take a nap?

BROKE BACK MOUNTAIN (CONDENSED)

Two cowboys went on horses,
Up Broke Back mountain way.
A herd of sheep went with em,
So they could earn some pay.
The night grew cold and stormy,
The whisky went right down.
The sheep were soon forgotten,
And blue jeans hit the ground.
What happened then's a puzzle,
They didn't go to sleep.
Inside that tent they frolicked,
And got in way too deep.
Now I ain't ever tried it,
So I don't really know.
I guess the sheep were ugly,
Or just no fun to blow.
But I can say for certain,
It takes a twisted dude,
To stick it in his buddies butt.
Hell, that's just downright rude.
There was an awful price to pay–
In morning air so still.
Their butts were sore and so they had
To walk back down the hill.
Then next year they went fishin
At least that was their line.

And when they grabbed each others rod,
It felt so firm and fine.
They frolicked in the meadow,
They frolicked in the grass.
They both risked everything they had
To get each others ass.
The piper soon they had to pay,
Their story ended sad.
Then Hollywood took up the tale
Of gay Wyoming lads.
Some folks cheered this love story,
But real men were pissed.
Up the butt was fine with them—
BUT DID THEY HAVE TO KISS!

CAN YOU DIG IT?

I dug a hole,
And threw in the shovel.
Kicked in the dirt,
And smoothed out the rubble.
Way down the road,
A thousand years hence.
It will be unearthed
At some great expense.
Archeologists then,
will ponder with trouble—
Why did some fool,
Bury a shovel?

CAT AT BAT

Two old men and one old cat,
Watched baseball on TV.
They asked the cat, "what inning?"
"I've not a clue," said he.
The three sat there in silence,
Transfixed upon the game.
Hey, tell me cat, what is the score?
Cats answer was the same.
Then tell me cat what is the count,
How many men on base?
The cat said that he didn't know,
And rubbed his whiskered face.
One man asked the other,
Just why is this cat here?
Because, his buddy answered,
He always brings the beer.

CHANCES ARE

I guess four aces
Is a pretty good hand.
But I wouldn't know
Cause I'm not a gambling man.
When it comes to health insurance
Well, I haven't got a plan.
But I see the doctor once a year,
Cause I'm not a gambling man.
I like to play the market
On margin when I can.
I love it out on Wall Street,
Cause I'm not a gambling man.
A lot of folks like playing cards,
But it really should be banned.
Cause gamblers lose out in the end,
And I'm not a gambling man.
Oh, sure I drive on freeways,
And going fast is grand.
But I don't like taking chances,
Cause I'm not a gambling man.

COMPUTER CAT

The cat, a stray,
Upon my laptop
Likes to play.
With reckless paws
She presses keys,
A windows wordsmith want to be.
I wonder will she
With her luck,
Step out a verse
That earns a buck.
With all her skill
At winning hearts,
Writing might
Just be her art.
Her random act
Though all by chance,
Might just earn
A critic's glance.
And if you will
Imagine that . . .
A Pulitzer
Prize winning cat.

CRYING WOLF

Ned always was a liar.
A teller of tall tales.
When his lips were moving,
Lies dropped out like hail.
And everybody knew it.
And so the doctor scoffed,
When Ned came in and told him,
"My death is three days off."
Ned died just two days later.
They buried him real quick.
Ned's tombstone bore his only truth:
"I told you I was sick."

DOWN LOAD

A million Chimps all typing,
For a million years or so.
Will write by chance a masterpiece.
(Or so the theory goes.)
But judging by the emails
From humans that I get.
The world wide web and internet,
Have not produced one yet.

FIXED

If it ain't broke don't fix it,
So the saying goes.
But I keep fixin things that work,
Why I just don't know.
Maybe its cause I'm a guy,
Or maybe I'm just dense.
Last week I fixed a thing that worked
And it ain't worked right since.

GENE POOL

I can't say I've ever seen Bigfoot.
I don't believe in him.
But I can say for certain—
I've met his next of kin!

GENOME

Genetics are a clever thing,
Which leads to this brain teaser.
If your folks never had a kid,
It's likely you won't either.

HANG IN THERE

If at first you don't succeed,
Well, welcome to the club.
I can't recall a first time,
When I didn't make a flub.
First marriage was a failure,
(I bet that yours was too.)
Got tangled up in knots,
First time I tied my shoe.
I failed at my first spelling test,
And algebra was worse.
In fact my all-time watch word is,
Rehearse rehearse rehearse.
My string of first time failures,
Could reach around the globe.
It hasn't gotten better,
As I have gotten old.
As proof this little ditty has
Been written out two times.
The first one was a failure,
But this one turned out fine.

HIGH SCHOOL REUNION

Went back to my reunion.
Was it that long ago,
When we were kids in high school?
My how the time has flown.
There's old Dave the football star,
No longer trim and fit.
He's boring me with stories bout,
His artificial hip.
My God can that be Sandy,
On whom I had a crush?
If she should trip and fall on me,
My bones would all be crushed!
With raspy voice and trembling hand,
The once class President,
Takes the mike and starts to speak,
He looks so tired and bent.
The super stars from yesterday,
It seems did not pan out.
Their pensions barely get them by,
They live a life of doubt.
The girls who once seemed homely,
Have blossomed now at last.
The prom night queen of yesterday,
Is fat and fading fast.
Who are all these old folks?
Is this a nursing home?
I think I see Rod Serling,
I'm in The Twilight zone!

IF YOU DIDN'T NEED THE MONEY

The money that we earn
Never seems to cure the yearn
Or scratch the itch
Or even sooth the burn.
We work hard just to retire
But our debts get even higher
Buying things we do not need
But somehow still require.
So . . .
If you didn't need the money would you do it?
Would you go to work each day or just say "screw it!"
Seems like all the bills we pay really never go away,
So it's pointless when you really come down to it.

KEEP IT SIMPLE STUPID

There is strength in brevity,
Fewer words are better.
Stripped of all verbosity,
Try not to be clever.

Simple words have power,
They penetrate the brain.
Big words don't communicate,
And have to be explained.

Simplicity ain't easy,
It's hard to write that way.
But keep it plain and simple.
You'll be a Hemingway.

LIFE'S LITTLE AGONIES

Life's little agonies
A curse of the old.
Ending up broke
In a climate that's cold.
A mate that don't love you
And kids that don't care.
Knees that won't bend
And losing your hair.
Wearing old clothes
That used to be hip,
Losing your hearing
And loosing your grip.
How could we know
In the days of our youth,
That being this old
Would be this uncouth.

MONSTER MASH

When I was just a little boy,
Each night I'd hide my head.
Beneath the covers cause a monster
Lived under my bed.
Though I had never seen it,
Twas there without a doubt.
The damn thing only came out when
The bedroom light was out.
Around my room it prowled about,
This awful ugly beast.
Knowing that my toes and ears
Would make a tasty feast.
In terror I would tremble neath
My snug Roy Rogers sheets.
And every time it made a sound,
My heart would skip a beat.
Some nights I'd leave the light on,
But dad would turn it out.
And once he shut my bedroom door,
The beast would slink about.
Then one day it dawned on me.
The problem was the bed.
The answer to the problem was
Out in my dad's shed.
It took a lot of effort but,
The beast at last has fled.
I got a little saw and sawed
The legs off of my bed.

PAPER OR PLASTIC?

I buy groceries too often,
So it's a decision I make everyday.
Am I saving the planet with plastic?
Or is paper the far better way?
A simple decision for many—
But a definite problem for me.
Do I fill up the landfill with plastic?
Or make paper bags out of trees?
The question comes, "paper or plastic?"
And the clerk isn't willing to guess.
I don't really know how to answer,
So I simply look up and say, "yes."

PHYSICS

The speed of light is established,
It's fast as the blink of an eye.
One eighty six thou miles per second,
There's nothing that faster can fly.
But then I got to thinking,
While walking in the park.
We know the speed of light,
But what's the speed of dark?

SIZE MATTERS

Golf balls are, well, golf ball size.
On that we all agree.
And grapefruit are much larger,
As they hang on the tree.
A baseball isn't quite as big,
A pebble even smaller.
And pellets are so tiny
They hardly even matter.
But pity the poor hailstone,
As earth it's soon to pelt.
It's size will be "reported"
As the size of something else.

SKY MILES

I am a frequent flyer,
And often have this dream;
The engines stop, we start to dive,
The passengers all scream.
Every wonder what you'd think about
As your last moments pass?
The last thing that goes through your mind,
Is probably your ass.

SPIN DOCTOR

The man himself doesn't interest us.
It's image we admire.
The aura that surrounds the man—
Of that we never tire.
Don't bore us with mere substance.
That's far too trite a thing.
It's superficiality
That gives him legs and wings.
Facts will come, then fade away,
Remembered by a few.
Contrived imagination—
That's what we love to view.

TAKING STOCK

Hickory dickory doc, the market just went flop.
Can all the stock brokers who come in at ten,
Put dot com back together again?

TAX TIME

I've created a pile of papers
On my dining room table today.
The 15th of April has hit me.
The tax man he cometh my way.
I look at the checks I have written.
The money has just flown away.
I search for each legal deduction,
So taxes I don't have to pay.
Can last year be over so quickly?
Can this year be already here?
The government asks for my money,
But the forms aren't terribly clear.
I wonder if maybe they'd listen
To something I just have to say.
If I have to live on a budget,
Why in the hell shouldn't they?

THE ANT AND THE GRASSHOPPER TODAY

The ant worked hard all last Summer,
Storing food for the winter away.
So that he would have some provisions
To eat on those cold winter days.
The grasshopper he saw things different,
Thought the ant was a rube and a fool.
With the weather so nice and sunny,
He preferred to lounge by the pool.
Sure enough one day it turned winter.
But the ant had planned far ahead.
Safe and warm in his ant hill he flourished,
While the grasshopper, well, he's near dead.
CNN came to cover the story
And they broadcast the grasshopper's fate.
They admonished the ant for his treasures,
And the food he had there on his plate.
Obama jumped into the action,
Demanding the poor ant pay up.
"He got rich on the back of the hoppers,
And now he has more than enough!"
Politicians soon heard the story
And desperate to get hopper votes,
They raided the ants little warehouse
And taxed away half of his oats.

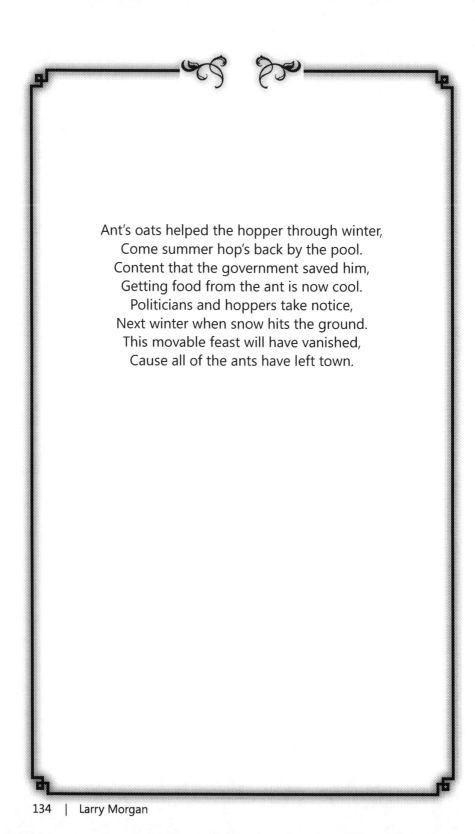

Ant's oats helped the hopper through winter,
Come summer hop's back by the pool.
Content that the government saved him,
Getting food from the ant is now cool.
Politicians and hoppers take notice,
Next winter when snow hits the ground.
This movable feast will have vanished,
Cause all of the ants have left town.

THE PARTIES OVER

Liberals Liberals everywhere,
As far as the eye can see.
Taxing away my money,
So others can live off of me.
The Bible thumping right
Is still trying to get my vote.
They shove their uptight morals,
Down my moderate throat.
The Left won't stay out of my checkbook.
The Right thinks my bedroom's their turf.
They talk but they never solve problems,
And our deficit keeps getting worse.
The "safety net" now is a hammock.
Illegals do all of our work.
Our dollar keeps getting weaker,
But unions still get all their perks.
I'm happy to pay my taxes,
And fight for my country and bleed.
But all of this Socialist bullshit,
Is something I simply don't need.
Let's stop foreign aid to all countries,
Whose dictators pillage and loot.
Stop voting for dumb politicians,
And then bring home all of our troops.

It's time we all take back our country,
The land of the free and the brave.
Or the government soon will make us,
The land of the weak and enslaved.
Stop voting for morons and scoundrels,
The next time you go to the poll.
Across the face of your ballot,
In bold letters simply right NO!
And the next time they ask for your taxes,
An I O U send their way.
If we have to live within budget,
Why in the hell shouldn't they?

THERE OUTTA BE A LAW

There outta be a law,
And I'm sure there probably is.
Like, you can't pull off the road
And leave your car and take a whiz.

You have to pay your taxes,
Though lots of people don't.
And you have to pay your bills,
But lots of people won't.

Mostly you cannot smoke pot,
Or drive and have a brew.
And mostly you just get one wife,
But in Utah some have two.

You have to stop at red lights,
But most of us roll thru.
You can't exceed the posted speed,
But seems we always do.

Yes, there outta be a law,
And I guess we should obey it.
But human nature tells us that,
It's lots more fun to break it.

THINK ABOUT IT

Its the early bird that gets the worm,
On that we all agree.
Wake up bright and early,
And fly down from that tree.
The bird that flies down first,
The worm he gets with ease.
It doesn't work that way for mice.
The second one gets the cheese.

TO HAVE AND TO HOLD

I have been a bachelor,
For nearly 30 years.
I've had a lot of good times,
I've also shed some tears.
And I've been all around the world,
On foot, by car and wing.
I've made a lot of money,
I own a lot of things.
And though I'm getting older,
And not still in my prime.
I still can ski black diamonds,
I hike, and bike, and climb.
I've done most of this solo,
Spent lots of time alone.
Time to settle down a bit,
And spend some time at home.
So now I need a woman,
Someone to have and hold.
One who's not too ugly,
And one who's not too old.
Be nice if she was sexy,
Could cook and clean and sew.
I might even marry her,
And leave her all my dough.

But pretty girls look thru me,
And old ones are too bold.
Young girls end up leaving you,
And wives grow fat and cold.
I've concluded after searching,
On line and in some bars,
That women ARE from Venus,
And me, well, I'm from Mars.
My mother always said that I
Would end up all alone,
How did mother get so smart,
When all I got was old?
Well maybe she is out there,
And maybe she is hot.
She's probably just like my ex,
But God I hope she's not.

WRITERS BLOCK

A romance novel,
Now that's real hot.
I just lack a title
And maybe a plot.
I'm sure that it's sexy,
Best seller for sure.
But the voice still escapes me,
And the words are a blur.
I picture the cover,
A scene in the mist.
Caught up in my arms,
She waits to be kissed.
The publishers waiting,
Big bucks on the line.
And going on tour,
Will really be fine.
But stop! There's a problem.
I have to admit.
I don't have a clue
As just how to write it.